CW01655843

Mummy's New Baby

Written by Nicola Fairbairn
Illustrated by Ruth Hearson

10

It was nearly the end of
the summer holidays.
In two weeks, Mummy was
going to have her new baby.

There was a lot
to get ready.

Mummy was washing
tiny pink vests and
baby grows.

Daddy was upstairs putting
the cot back together.

Joshua was sorting out some of his soft toys for his new baby sister.

But Rosie was
sitting under the
kitchen table.

"What are you doing under there Rosie?" asked Daddy when he came downstairs to make a cup of tea.

"I'm thinking,"
Rosie said sadly.

"What about?"
said Daddy.

"I'm thinking
that once the
baby comes,
there might not
be much room
in this family
for me."

Daddy smiled a big kind smile, "Oh Rosie, that's definitely not true!"

"Why not?" she asked.

"We may be getting another little girl in our family, but she won't ever replace you. You are special."

He reached up to the shelf

and took out the Bible.

Then he climbed under the table next to Rosie.

"Let's see what God has to say about you."

Daddy opened up the Bible to the book of Psalms.

Psalm 139:14–16

I praise you because you made me
in an amazing and wonderful way.
What you have done is wonderful.
I know this very well.
You saw my bones being
formed as I took shape
in my mother's body.

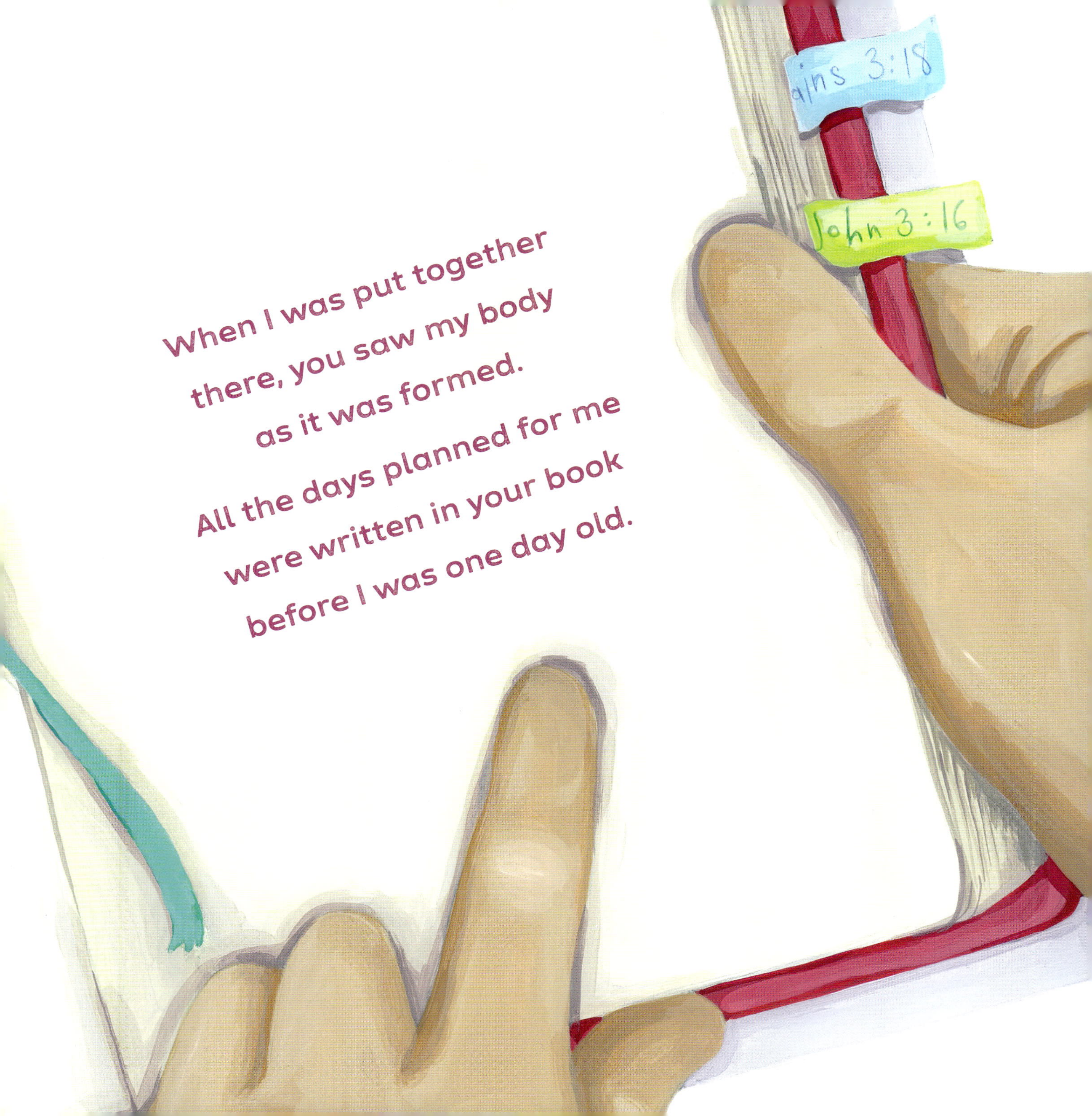

When I was put together
there, you saw my body
as it was formed.
All the days planned for me
were written in your book
before I was one day old.

"You see Rosie, God made you in an amazing way and there is no one else quite like you.

And now your job is to be a kind big sister to our new baby."

Rosie smiled. “Yes, I see.”

Then they prayed to thank God for making everything and everyone so well.

Two and a half weeks later,

baby Abigail was born.

When Mummy came home from the hospital, Rosie was allowed to cuddle her new sister on the sofa.

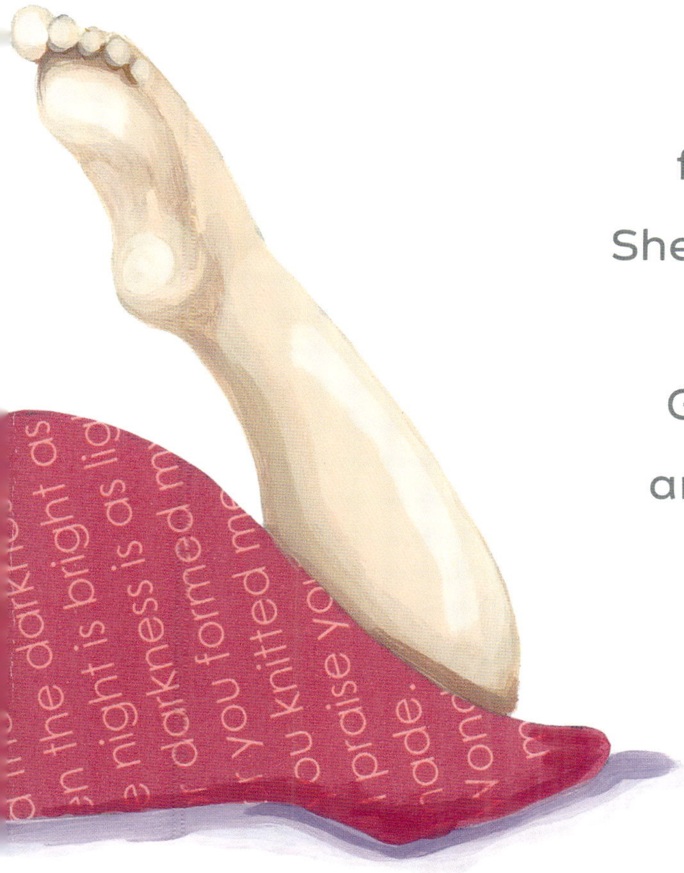

She looked at Abigail's tiny fingers and cute little nose. She smiled at her and whispered into her ear, "Wow Abigail, God has made us both in an amazing and wonderful way."

For Ibby – NF

For the lovely Hibberts family – RH

Mummy's New Baby

Published by 10Publishing, a division of 10ofThose Limited.

ISBN: 978-1-912373-72-7

Typeset by Diane Warnes
Printed in the UK

10Publishing, a division of 10ofthose.com
Unit C, Tomlinson Road, Leyland, Lancashire, PR25 2DY England
Email: info@10ofthose.com
Website: www.10ofthose.com